WRITE THE WRONGS

Milo & Jarvie

Nothing is impossible

All poems © Kimba
Illustrations by Joseph Witchall

ISBN : 978-1-9196148-2-3

First published in 2022
by Caboodle Books

All rights reserved. Apart from any use permitted under UK copyright law, this publication may only be reproduced, stored or transmitted, in any form, or by any means, with prior permission in writing from the publishers or in the case of reprographic production in accordance with the terms of licences issued by the Copyright Licensing Agency, and may not be otherwise circulated in any form of binding or cover other than that in which it is published and without a similar condition being imposed on the subsequent purchaser.

A Catalogue record for this book is available from the British Library.
Page Layout by Highlight Type Bureau Ltd, Leeds LS20 8LQ
Printed and bound by by CPI Group (UK) Ltd, Croydon, CR0 4YY

The paper and board used in this book are natural recyclable products made from wood grown in sustainable forests. The manufacturing processes conform to the environmental regulations of the country of origin.

MIX
Paper from responsible sources
FSC® C171272

Caboodle Books Ltd.
Riversdale, 8 Rivock Avenue,
Steeton, BD20 6SA, UK.

Dedication

I dedicate this book to my family. Firstly to my lovely young family of Susie, Ezra, and Indigo. You are amazing beyond words. Your love helps me fulfill my life's greatest potential.

Secondly to my Bush and Ramsey family. Your enduring love gives me a foundation to grow from and exceed any limits of expectation. I hope I make you proud.

Thank You To:

Karl Nova I remember the first time I saw you perform in London. I knew you were special and I hoped we'd get to work together one day. I never knew the bridge you would become in my life. From the depths of my heart, thank you bro. I'm so happy to see you soar and look forward to that continuing.

Yvonne, Robin, Trevor, Angela, and the entire Authors Abroad organization it has been amazing to work with you, a dream come true really. Thank you for all the opportunities, confidence in me, and support. I really appreciate it. Cheers to the future.

To the amazing Joseph Witchall thank you for bringing my vision to life through your illustrations. Your work is one of my life's greatest experiences. I love it. Thank you.

To my brother DeMond, thank you for your love, every word and experience we've ever shared. You are one of the greatest people to have ever lived on this planet. The inspiration you give is limitless. Cheers to the future.

Mom, thank you so much. I hope to write many more words for you.

Dad, thank you so much. I hope to write many more words for you.

Geoff and Dee Anderson thank you so much. Your enduring love and support has been beyond anything I could have ever asked or expected.

My dear Bishop Noel McLean & the YCF family you made this American boy feel right at home. Thank you for showing me what a spiritual family is. You've given me an international heritage.

Kwaku and Ms Serwah it has been an honour to receive your embrace and be able to support BTWSC and all your amazing endeavours. Cheers to the future.

ACKNOWLEDGEMENTS

To every school I've had the honour of working with or will soon through Authors Abroad, thank you for making my dreams come true. Using my gifts to inspire, educate, and empower young people has been a childhood ambition. To now do so through writing, poetry, and music fulfills me exponentially. My journey is living proof to all students, parents, teachers, and community organizations that as a global community we can produce resilient, creative success stories regardless of starting points. I hope this book does for your pupils what my first reading experiences did for me at the public library in Frankfort, Ky, USA.

I appreciate you all. I must acknowledge a few who especially inspired and encouraged me in my initial Authors Abroad visits.

Sabrina Munday, Head Librarian at St. Albans girls prep (STAHS). From our initial car journey conversation and my visit it became clear my journey as a writer, facilitator, and performer was entering a beautiful new world of literary appreciation. Your feedback continues to fuel my journey.

Atiya Bauer, Head Librarian at the John Whitgift School, the prestige, appreciation and humility of Whitgift will forever remain with me. Your reception of me, and the conversations we had with some of the boys in the library after assembly has affirmed my artistic passion as much as anything I've ever experienced.

Chris Peake, Primary English Leader at Eastbrook School in Dagenham your love for your students was amazing. Your staff and students' engagement set a standard for me of what a school visit can produce.

Luke Evans, Head of Year 10 and Drama at The Warriner School our personal rapport felt like an old friendship. Thank you for sharing your journey with me and for allowing me to invest in the students at Warriner. It was a pleasure to see the diversity of personalities, talents, and gifts there. I'll never forget that moment when that young man sat down to accompany me on piano for his first ever impromptu live performance. Hopefully that will be a great turning point for him. And I've become a student of Lin Manuel Miranda since you introduced me to Hamilton. Thank you.

Finally to Aimee Coombs, Head of English at Claremont Fan Court School, thank you. Your warm reception was amazing, as well as the staff and students so engaging. The student enthusiasm and work continues to inspire me. Your feedback on the day continues to increase my hopes and expectations of poetry's potential in early academia.

Contents

	Page
Boom	7
Dandy Lion	10
Toe Food	12
Choppers	14
Cerita The Cheetah	16
Pen A Trait	18
Young Navigators	20
Hooper Troopers	23
Chalk	25
Word Play	27
Decipher	29
Night Lights	31
Use Your Noodles Ricely	33
Imagine Nation	34
Shore Thing	37
The Bait Escape	38
Memory Bank	40
Big Inside	42
Prints Charming	43
Lip Service	46
Class Bloom	48
Face My Fears	50
Currency	52
Memory Lane	54
Caught In The Brainstorm	56
Steam	58
Roots To The Sky	60
Food For Thought	62
Know It All	64
In Pulses	66
Bridges	68

Glass Ceiling	70
Words Worth	73
Master Key	75
Maple Cheeks	77
Hope Less	79
Legends	81
Text Yours	83
Writers Block	85
Charlie Brown	87
Eye See You	89
Heir Born	91
Speechless	93
Free Air	95
Bubble Guts	97
Habit To Grab It	100
Head In The Clouds	102
Hair Dues	104
Chasing The Wind	107
Street English	110
Evolution	113
Prescription	114
Apples	116
Big Wheels	118
Hue Man	120
The Moors	122
Pitch Perfect	124
She Rules	126

Boom

Boom clack boom boom boom clack
Boom clack boom boom boom clack
Boom clack boom boom boom clack
When I first heard this I said what's that

It went

Boom clack boom boom boom clack
Boom clack boom boom boom clack
Boom clack boom boom boom clack
When I first heard this I said what's that

the pound of the drum
roared out the windows
from cars on our road
a fire was kindled
deep in my heart
that crackled to the tempo
of a sound I'd never heard
a voice and instrumental
It was a kick drum
hi hat then a snare
a deep bass sound
so sweet to my ears
I nodded my head
there was something in the air
energy hit my body
it became quite clear
I needed to be a part of this
not just in the audience
I saw myself writing rhymes
started targeting
thoughts and ideas I could share
it was marvellous
a new way to express myself
in a song that went

Boom clack boom boom boom clack
Boom clack boom boom boom clack
Boom clack boom boom boom clack
When I first heard this I said what's that

It went

Boom clack boom boom boom clack
Boom clack boom boom boom clack
Boom clack boom boom boom clack
When I first heard this I said what's that

the rhythm and rhyme
tickled my spine
lyrical lines
they settled inside
deep in my mind
I memorised
in the quickest of time
what I would hear
then design
something unique and different
but totally all mine
flowing like ocean water
my tongue that was tied
Roared like some waves
rising like the tides
on shores of creativity
I stood so surprised
ready to go as deep as I could
I took a dive
into

Boom clack boom boom boom clack
Boom clack boom boom boom clack
Boom clack boom boom boom clack
When I first heard this I said what's that

It went

Boom clack boom boom boom clack
Boom clack boom boom boom clack
Boom clack boom boom boom clack
When I first heard this I said what's that

Quite some time ago as I walked through my neighbourhood I could hear the sound of something I'd never heard before coming out of car speakers. It wasn't singing. It was rhythmic talking over music with rhymes all throughout. It had a lot of different emotions in it. The music as well had a different sound. It wasn't something I could just ignore, it captured and commanded my attention. As I listened more I could hear people sharing familiar experiences and dreams to mine. The more I heard it the more I wanted to try it. At first it was artists called Slick Rick and Dana Dane. Then it was LL Cool J. Then it was The Fresh Prince of Bel Air and Vanilla Ice. Eventually there were a whole list of artists that inspired me to pick up a pen and start writing lyrics that made me feel valuable, that I had something to say the world would want to hear. Once I got familiar with the art of rhyming and performing poems and songs I was hooked. I started writing everyday.

Dandy Lion

That flower has an Afro
We used it to decorate the air
When we blew it
soft or hard
It shared all of its hair
We ran into the field
there were so many there
Mother Earth at spring time
had an expression so rare
reds and blues
yellows, purples, whites
so many hues
fields full of grasshoppers
and crickets singing nature's glorious tunes
but this one particular flower
kept our attention
had us amused
The one we picked the most
the first we'd ever choose
no amazing colour
no amazing smell
but fascinating still
a puff ball with no gel
the sunflower is bright
and roses are gorgeous
But as children we found
this flower with white afro
the most important
Fluff in the air
We'd puff then stare
Watch them drift away
Sun in the sky
clouds so high
For hours we'd spend in a day
Welcome to our world

This flower introduced us
To a love of nature
We'd have well into our future

This flower to me is one of Earth's wonders. It is so unique and simple. It invites us to establish a relationship with plants like none other. Most flowers are picked to smell or put in pots and watch grow. This one says pick me, hold me, give me a push from the breath of your lungs and watch me fill the air. My brother and I didn't often pick flowers when we were young. But we did this one. Sometimes we'd race to see who could pick the closest one first or blow out the most the quickest. It's funny how simple and fun it was and still is actually. But sometimes I feel sorry for them and wonder is that really what they were meant for.

Toe Food

Drop kicks and chopsticks
captivated our conscious
Saturday mornings were for doughnuts and milk
martial arts and shadow boxing
kung fu matinee cartoons
Shaolin monks kept us watching
fist of fury, enter the dragon
the crane, the tiger, techniques and options
who would rule the day
With their toes or their fists
Fighting was an art form
Martial artists gave a twist
Numb chucks or the katana
Throwing stars in our pyjamas
We joined the ranks of ninjas
Graced tops of buildings
Sparred in honour
Of this eastern heritage
You would have thought we were adopted
Eastern culture raised us
fed our souls through our sockets
We were sold we were locked in
kicks and punches that popped chins
our street was our dojo
with our friends we'd plot to win
train then watch again
to perfect our meditation
the calm of the conqueror
We spoke about in conversation
Our horse stance
our legs spread, feet flat
one palm facing out
the other tucked in a fist underarm
moved swiftly forward
with a quicker breath from the mouth

We were mastering motivation
from right outside the house
our neighbourhood feeding our imagination
to outsiders food unannounced
A cultural buffet this smorgasbord
The art of war
discipline and diligence
for young hearts so pure
We grew through every session
our young hearts matured
our love for the language of movement
our young smarts adored
we were transported to another world
our young hearts explored
the start of a life long journey
this art was a door

Growing up on the east coast of the US every Saturday morning the Kung Fu cartoon theatre show would come on for at least two hours. My brother and I would be right there in front of the TV to watch every minute of it. Our Mom used to get us donuts on those mornings. So Saturdays were a really big deal. To have donuts, cold milk to dip them in, and Kung Fu cartoons was paradise for us. This is when we developed a great love for martial arts and Bruce Lee. We never officially took a class. But nearly everyday we'd practise on each other or our neighbourhood friends. We were even allowed to stay up some nights and climb up on the rooftops of buildings and re-enact scenes from ninja films. One of our latino friends Rueben actually had a family member who trained as a ninja. Once he invited us over to see some of the kit. There was a ninja suit hung on the wall and many of the weapons they use, throwing stars, katanas, numb chucks, and different lengths of swords. Those times were amazing. We loved the idea and art of being a skilful artistic fighter who could save the day. When the rap group from New York City, Wu Tang Clan came out in the 90s I could see where they got their influence from. I didn't know it at the time. But New York City was only about two and a half hours from Trenton, New Jersey where we lived. Kung Fu and martial arts had a great impact on the east coast and us.

CHOPPERS

Bikes were meant to be ridden
Not treated like gymnasts
Unfortunately that's what happened
When I developed too much momentum
It was my favourite hill
practically no wind resistance
which is why
My heels went over my head
When I flipped it
I had persisted with vision
to a hill top
at great distance
from the peak of its summit
to the bottom
to risk this
reaching a great speed
pushing all the physics
My little body could achieve
through scientific mischief
I set off with a push
Squeezing the grips
feet pushing pedals
poking out my lips
my butt above my head
near handle bars
downward I sped
in the middle of the road
on a residential street
cars became a blur
trees and speech
clothes flapping in the wind
against my body they beat
til the curb gashed open my wrist
barely missing my teeth

Before Harleys it was BMX
Mags and pegs kept it fresh
Pop a wheelie down the boulevard
Right through traffic life at threat
Many would take the risk
To prove who was the best
But after I hit that curb
I laid all that to rest

Bikes were a big deal to us growing up, ten speeds, mountain bikes, and especially the American brands called BMX and Huffy dirt bikes. People who could do the most stunts were popular in the neighbourhood. Everyday you'd see someone riding down on the back wheel of a bike trying to ride the entire length of a street. There were constant competitions. One of those competitions was to see who could jump the highest off a ramp. So we used to find materials and build them as big as we could to do the biggest stunt. We would also try to find the steepest roads in town to ride down the fastest during races. Once I tried this on my own. As the poem says it didn't end too well for me. I still have the scar on my left wrist to prove it. It was the fastest I'd ever travelled down a hill on a bike and I almost finished it. But at the last minute my left foot slipped off the pedal and I couldn't get control of my speed. At that point I panicked and started to wobble the handlebars a bit. Next thing I knew my head was going over top of the handle bars headed towards a curb. Thankfully my wrist was the only part I injured. And the owner of the house where I landed came out to check on me as she must have seen me take the tumble. That was my last high speed attempt. I became a cruiser after that. I appreciated the stunts others could do. But my accident seemed too dangerous for me to risk repeating. Although I did still like the BMX freestyle stunts with pegs on the front and back wheels, as well as kitting out your wheels with five star rims and all that stuff.

CERITA THE CHEETAH

She was a cheetah
Easily spotted in our city for her speed
The track team had stars
But she was from another planet
No one could see her
when she took off
she did damage
To what we thought
girls could do
Boys ate the dust off her feet
The souls of her shoes
Flattened them one by one
Til there was none left
In each crew
Boys were no competition
Though they often tried
Victory after victory
She softened the toughest guys
If you thought you could take her
You were in for a rough ride
This feline was so stream lined
And had so much pride
A champion of sorts
She had no remorse
In leaving the hopes of boys
Stiff as a corpse
The hunter the predator
She was always on course
She had the eye of the tiger
And opponents hearts on a fork

One of the fastest people in our city was a fifteen year old girl from my neighbourhood called Cerita Osborne. To this day I remember seeing her catch and surpass a girl three quarters of a lap ahead of her in a relay race to win a championship. It was often unbelievable how fast she was. People used to assume that boys were always faster than girls. Cerita changed that in our neighbourhood. Not many people wanted to race her and when they did many were embarrassed. I learned a lot from her actually looking back. She loved running, and competition. She was fearless and confident in her ability.

Pen A Trait

If I could penetrate the sky
with a pencil I'd try
to draw energy from the sun
and write letters that could fly
carrying sunbeams across
a darkened world wide
Through photosynthesis
Nurture dreams
Others have inside

Each stroke of my pen
Would reflect as a mirror
Where people could see
their dreams, and visions much clearer
Their gifts and abilities
From their crowns to their toes
The power at their finger tips
Waiting to explode

I've heard words paint pictures
and grow as seeds
In peoples minds like gardens
I'll sow flowers not weeds

Til from towers
We see leaves
Above our heads
Helping us breathe
And they wave inviting me back
To harvest fruit
From their trees

I would penetrate
Write til my pencil breaks
And shatters every condition
That cripples our mental state

I would write til my pencil shapes
A glorious mental space
And we all feel like astronauts
Exceeding limits of weight

I'd pen til my pencil's properties
Changes the world's biology
Settle the scores of wars
And for the poor to live properly
Earth is a big place
There's more than enough property
So when I pen
I birth traits
Hoping that people copy me

As I've grown as a writer and performer over the years I've realised the power writing has to change ourselves and others. Writing like farming is the practice of sowing seeds of thought that can grow over time to produce different behaviours that can nurture people's progress. Here I explore the nature of doing that. With a pen I penetrate the mind with words that reproduce fruitful thoughts. As a performer as well it's always amazing when people speak to you after hearing a piece to confirm how beneficial and empowering your words were for them. How what you've written has influenced them to do the same.

Young Navigators

We were
Too young to drive
Yet we knew the roads
The city was large
but it was ours
We knew it loads
Alleyways, parks, and corner-shops
street names and post codes
especially if we had relatives there
we'd spend nights
barrow clothes
Played ninjas on Calhoun Street
hit the pool at Catwater Park
Ate snow cones at George Washington Monument
during heritage day
face painting and art
music filled the air
colours bright as rainbows
downtown was cotton candy
after bus rides
grabbing bagels
The unknown was our familiar
Me and my big brother
Lifetime explorers
We loved to discover
Trenton New Jersey
our beautiful city
Some called it the gutter
But our imaginations flowed through it
without even a stutter
hear the bat crack
in an early morning baseball match
yellow team shirt
socks up to your knees
leather glove and matching hat
ball flying towards the fence

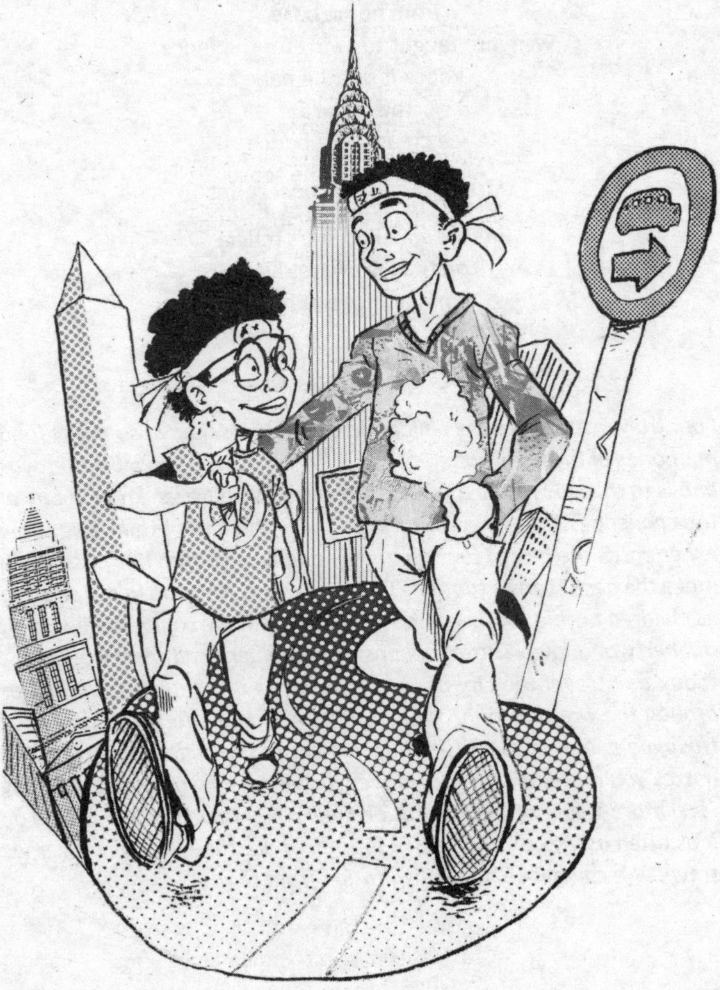

who could steel the home run
with a catch
the roar of parents and family
from the sidelines
as the sun tanned our flesh
from home base
we were taught to swing for the fence
knock it out the park
the reward
ice cream on a bench
All of it gave us the sense
Of where we could go in life
As we watched stars reflect
on the Delaware river
From a bridge at night

I am truly grateful for my childhood experiences. I have so many fond memories of my family and the city we grew up in. My big brother was and is to this day my best friend. Although I didn't even know many of the challenges that faced our family then. The more I think about my experiences the more I love my family and believe that it is possible to make the best of any situation. There was so much to do in our city and as children my big brother and I did as much as we could. We had a lot of liberty and love. Those feelings of excitement still run through me today as I travel the city of London where I currently live and cities around the world through work and with family. Lately I've read that traveling is one of the best ways to increase intelligence as traveling makes you more sensitive to your environments. I would definitely say I feel more aware of the inspiration I feel when traveling. We should do it as often as we can and keep a journal of our thoughts whenever we travel. We can get so much inspiration from that.

HOOPER TROOPERS

The battlefield out back
Made men of us early
We took to it daily
Rain, sleet, or snow hurling
Our hands wrapped around
The precious game of life
Between lines facing netted hoops
We learned to fight
To go to war for rank
With valour in Nikes
To just do what we learned
Take off in flight
Perfecting our strike
In cross overs & step backs
A quick first step
To blow by opponents
Like jet packs
Crossover pull back
Fire long range jump shots
from the three point line
or backing opponents down
on the block
a drop step a pump fake
make them jump into the sky
then under the defenders arms
around their body
to put the ball in the net
and secure the win
for our posse
B Ball was life
We balled til sunset
Dreamed about it
Then wake up
To become a threat
On any court we touched
Aiming to be the best

Giving our all to the game
Till we had nothing left
We left it all on the court
Like any service vet

Sports was and is still a way of life for my family. Sports taught us so much about life. Discipline, hope, hard work, team work, community and overcoming adversity. I can't imagine my life without sports and am thankful to have grown up playing all the sports I did especially basketball. I've probably watched over a thousand hours of basketball games in my life because we loved and played it so often. Much of my character and charisma is a result of what I've learned about myself and others playing sports. It was only right that I share my love for basketball in this poem.

CHaLk

I hated school
My grades were low
My reading slow
And it was too competitive
Until the spelling competition came
and I finally saw some evidence
Of something I thought I lacked
I saw my own intelligence
how quick my brain could work
To solve problems then I was well convinced
Learning is fun
And it's good to have a challenge
Because my brain learns how to
Work through, over, or around it

It wasn't education I hated
I couldn't see how I was gifted
So in the frame work of school
I felt I was a misfit
But once I saw where mine existed
Everywhere I went I was learning
From second street to Conway avenue
I was spelling out wording
Something was ignited
Some how I felt more connected
And my classroom extended beyond
The brick building where I'd been taking lessons
Life became a classroom
And each day was study and testing
I started learning on the fly
Life was more interesting

One of the most significant occurrences in my life was winning the 7th grade spelling competition at my school, for which I received a trophy. I still remember the word I spelled wrong that put me out. It was exaggerate. I remember using phonics techniques to try and figure it out. Ex , a , ger , ate. I'm pretty sure I left out one of the g's. Even though I didn't win the entire competition all the way up to 8th grade, the level I achieved gave me confidence that I could do well at school and in life. I believe this also initiated my love for words. Words became fun for me. Knowing how to spell, writing words, learning new ones and expanding my vocabulary became exciting tasks.

Word Play

Writing is lovely
Seeing words on a page
Each one is an actor
They belong on a stage
Conveying a message
Once you get past the phrase
They want to leave a picture
That last in your mind
As frames

So I write a lot
To hit the spot when I jot
So every line & title
Is on point like a dot

Connecting every idea
That forms into a plot
my audience can see
like a screen they would watch

Act two scene one
backstage on the drum

The pauses the inflections
The tone from the tongue
plays a large part
Even a pause or a hum
Speeding up or slowing down
Taking a breath
Filling lungs

the tone is subjective
aspects of creativity
that turn poems into perfection
Props up your ability

To draw people in
Or out of the vicinity
Of our current world
Through word play and imagery

A picture's worth a thousand words
A thousand words are like a symphony
When they harmonise
We see life in sounds differently
So can you hear the music
In the rhythm and words
If you can
You can flip the script
To a tune you prefer

We all write the stories of our own lives. This is done with words and actions. I learned this from writing my first poetic journal entry when I was about eleven years old. Then I grew more aware of my love for music, and eventually my love of poetry through a film called Slam. I saw how words opened doors even in just daily conversations. When we share ideas we are sharing energy and inspiration that can change the course of our lives. Discovering how artists from different disciplines such as singing, rapping, and performance poetry all used words in unique ways made me love creativity. It made me appreciate how stringing the same words together in different ways can allow anyone to discover their creative genius. So everyday now I'm always discovering mine. I love writing.

DECIPHER

Observe these words
And the mental images they create
Are you able to interpret
the message they make

Rhymes through see to
World new whole a there's cause
Mind your open gotta just you
Do to easy it's but
Line same the in all fire and wind, earth put
Time same the at water like flow and
Flames speak I that
Surprising so it's some to so
Flames the out put to
Hydrant a provide then
Body my in fire me give they
Them try to love I
Sizes all of words
Words little
Words big

Big words
Little words
Words of all sizes
All sound good to me
I love to try them
They give me fire in my body
Then provide a hydrant
To put out the flames
So to some it's so surprising
that I speak flames
and flow like water at the same time
put earth wind and fire all in the same line
But it's easy to do
you just gotta open your mind
Cause there's a whole new world
to see through rhymes

This poem was an experiment. I wanted to see if a piece could communicate as effectively if the words were inverted. It's a sort of mental exercise. So I memorised and first performed this poem at the PopUp children's book festival held at The Waddesdon Manor in Aylesbury, England. The task I set for the audience was to write down each word I said in order and try to figure out what was being communicated. It was amazing to see the smiles on faces as some people were deciphering each line without being given clues to how the words had been arranged. People enjoyed the task of trying to figure out what the poem was communicating. After a ten minute deciphering session the task was complete. We all enjoyed seeing how the arrangement of words paint pictures in our minds, and even when not arranged properly our minds work to figure out what is trying to be communicated. It also re-emphasised how the precise arrangement of words clarify our communication.

NIGHT LIGHTS

Peering into night sky
They peer back
Silent as air
Whispering a confirming fact
Just beyond reach
Just beyond lack
Is abundance present
Hugely untapped
From continuing to stare
At lights with no switches
Hung on no fixtures
Plugged in to no source man made
In a space with no walls
nor floors at all
Fixed over time they remain
So as they watch me
I reflect
and put my dreams on a page
Dreaming in the dark
To find my form and a flame
that one day
They can light the world
As lamps on a stage

The natural elements of our universe are wonderfully mind stretching phenomenons. As we search to find explanations of how and why they exist we are stretched even further. In this piece I thought about the stars in space that light up our night time sky and how humanity has learned to tap into electricity. We have created lights we control with the use of wires and switches. But stars exist without any of those and stay lit for years remaining visible from millions of miles away. It is mind stretching to even think about. What else is there for us to tap in to? Through science we are learning so much about our untapped human abilities and the universe we live in. Did you know it is estimated that the human mind has at least 30,000 - 50,000 thoughts a day. So metaphorically we could compare our minds to the sky and our thoughts to the stars in the sky or space.

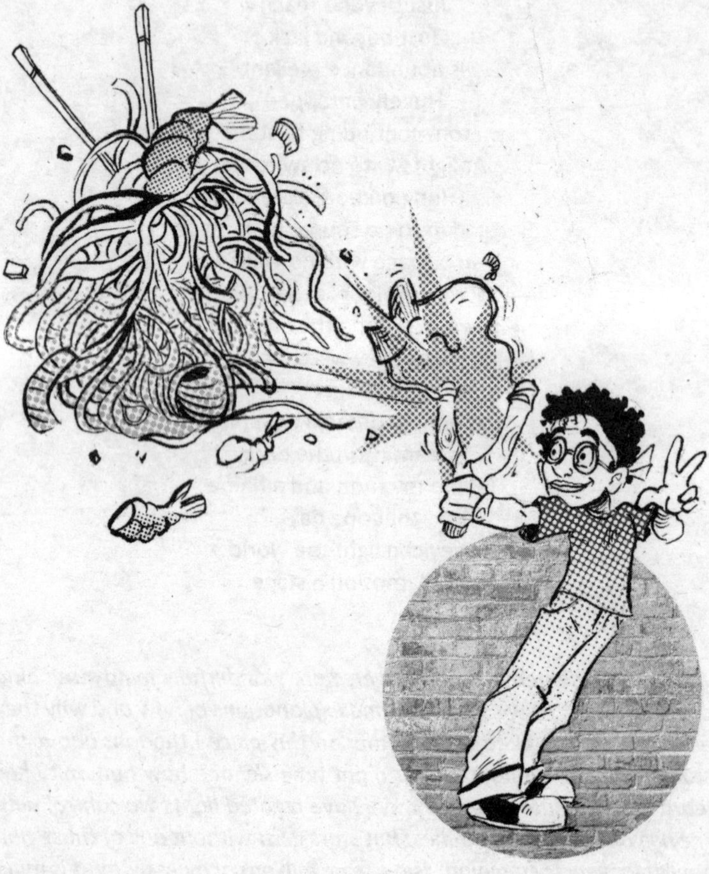

USE YOUR NOODLES RICELY

Teriyaki tortellini
Sushi shaki and zucchini
alfredo sauce and fettuccine
Sukiyaki manicotti kiwi
soups and salads
sides of seaweeds
Soba noodles and Sashimi
stocks in pots
wash it feed me
seasoned up I'll gobble it easy
linguine panini rigatoni stelline
strozzapreti, spaghetti, fregola, anelli
Ravioli, guacomole, stromboli, linguine
Let's head to the kitchen
I'll let you lead me
Cause
Tagliatelle is good for the belly
the garlic and onions they can be smelly
but seasoned just right
I know what you'll tell me
Using your noodles ricely
can keep you healthy

I love food and words. They are one and the same for me. Food feeds the body words feed the mind. So I wanted to combine them in rhyme. Lol..! It's amazing how culture is represented so vibrantly in food. Growing up we were exposed to a few different cultures, and heard this saying often to ' use your noodles ', which meant to use your mind to find solutions to problems or issues. So in this piece I tried to use as many of them as I could along with rice another household staple in a lot of countries. Italian and Oriental foods are actually two of my favourites. So writing this piece was great fun and it makes me hungry every time I read it.

Imagine Nation

Imagine this
the pencil that you hold
could create anything silver or gold
a car a phone
a pizza or ice cream in a cone
what would you create first
this is the power of writing poems
a power to some unknown
to pull swords from stones
take down big dragons
or tickle funny bones
til people wobble like noodles
cooked for too long
and they can no longer stand
from laughing it's too strong
that they turn into a puddle
on the floor
just used clothes
is all that's left of them
from laughing
they're truly gone

see these pencils we hold
have the power to create
the world we imagine
this wonderful place
full of playgrounds and parks
fish and chips, cupcakes
there's so much I could write
that it keeps me up late

You gotta love the world we live in
it's full of adventures and dreams
So where does yours start
what's the place
the scene

is it your kitchen cupboards
the closet
the room where you sleep
that has a doorway to a universe
you can escape to for weeks
mine was the American football pitch
and the basketball court
I studied moves players made
like naval sergeants set up forts
a pilot on the pitch
I would dazzle with my feet
Soar through the air
to catch balls out of reach
a warrior on the pitch
in my kit I was unleashed
like eagles
A wild thing
no player could tame or teach
a cat without a hat
I was fleet, I did feats
I had riddles, I had giggles,
I was nimble, I was neat
I confess, I made a mess,
It was fun, It was a feast
my imagination was hungry
as a caterpillar to eat

The Chronicles of Kimba
The football, the basketball, and the pen
this was my playground
a world without end
I had dreams
To create scenes
from under my eyelids
I had seen
So when I woke up
I was bursting at the seams
like Charlie with a golden ticket
to see chocolate flowing as streams

What I'd write
gave me life
for you
it will do the same thing

The pencil is one of humanity's greatest inventions. It's really our first recording device. It's how we first made a record of information either in drawings or words. And it is still as significant. We should all acknowledge the power of our pens or pencils in changing the world. Anybody can do it. From the moment we are inspired if we capture that in writing or drawing it can inspire generations of people. That's what museums are. They exhibit the ideas artists captured in history to inspire us to do the same now. I hope that this book will inspire its readers to write, to draw, to sing, to pursue whatever dreams that continue to speak to them daily. If we have a reoccurring desire that inspires us in spite of how impossible it might seem, it's probably a dream asking us to believe it's possible. I can say for sure that I never dreamed I'd live in another country. But my dreams of being an American footballer, a music artist and writer have given me a life beyond my original dreams and expectations. If and when we write and dream the possibilities are endless.

SHORE THING

From miles away
salt seasoned the air
Whetting our appetite over moments we'd share
Forever
Faces I can't recall
But the feelings are always present when I fall
into despair
The roar of those peaceful waves
The bare soles of my feet engraved
By the moist sand
Sun rays tingling my back
Restoring my youth
My hands
wrinkled from hours in the ocean relaxed
a bit tanner than days prior
This place I still admire
like great parents
Dreams were born in me here
On those rough shores
My heart softened by seagulls cries
The endless possibilities of empty coastlines
Sea breeze and blue skies
Being here breeds new eyes
I want to see again

It seems like I should've become a fishermen, a marine, or boat captain from how much I love the beach. The sun, the water, and sand have always made me love life so much. This poem is taken from childhood memories of my primary school taking us on yearly trips to the beach while we lived in our hometown of Trenton, New Jersey. It was amazing to take that trip every year. It was always fun and games, and great food. Those were my first experiences of the beach. So I have always loved it. One day I would like to live near the beach. I can only imagine the amazingly creative stuff I could write there. I think everyone feels this way about the beach. But maybe I'm wrong.

THE BAIT ESCAPE

Sun-kissed young skin
Eyes peering through murky water
With great anticipation
They hoped to see the aura
Of these phenomenal beings
Who breathe and are a source of
food and fascination
As they swim past their lures strung

As youngsters they were blessed with a Vietnamese guide
To teach them the art of preparing their lines
Preparing their souls for the process of patience
To catch something that held their young imaginations

On the banks of the Kentucky
They were River rats young and hungry
Appetites whet
eager for tasting
the fruits of their learning
and their labours

If ignorance was bliss
This was their foundation
On it they stood strong
Building dreams without hesitation

For several years of our childhood we lived on housing estates. One amazing aspect of housing estate lifestyle is usually the great diversity in the culture of people that live there. And we got to experience that first hand. We had a lovely Vietnamese neighbour named Wong who used to take me and my older brother fishing during the summer. As I mentioned before I've always grown up around rivers. While living in Frankfort, Kentucky the river was about a 10 minute walk for us and fishing was free. So we were able to fish as much as we wanted to as long as we knew how, had an adult with us and had the necessary equipment. Wong had everything we needed. So he used to take us all the time. Not only did he teach us how to catch fish, he showed us how to clean them and he cooked them as well. Our Mom was great at cooking as well. So she'd fry fish and we loved it. For the most part it was great. But Wong used to make this fish head soup that didn't smell so nice. One day we visited him and he let us look in the pot when he was cooking, only for us to see the heads of the fish in the pot, eyeballs and all. That was a bit much for us. We never ate that soup. But we loved Wong and spending time with him.

Memory Bank

We never talked about money
How we didn't have enough
Mom cooked, we ate
We played sports
Enjoyed being rough

Before I knew what poor meant
That we lived in poverty
We found joy in little things
Laughed at life
Like comedy

We laughed we smiled we cried
Scarred our bodies, we got bruised
Mom worked we watched
We learned over time
life has rules

When hard times came like strong winds
We had roots
We didn't move
We were planted in what she gave us
Clear in our views

It's expensive to build
Later in life we learned
The smallest early investment
Can have the greatest return

You see when you leave home
Home never leaves you
It's what helps you steer forward
As it remains in your rear view

I wasn't born into a financially wealthy family. But I was born into a family rich in love. And that's what they gave us. My mom made us feel so valuable. One day I may write an entire book about her. She deserves it. She was an amazing example of a hard working person for me to watch. Wise, courageous, sweet, intelligent, and beautiful she made us laugh so hard, made sure we were giving our all at school and sports, and that we were staying out of trouble. I know a large part of why I am the person I am today is because of the person she was then and still is. Enough can't be said of our parents efforts to give us a great start in life. Life is never perfect. But what we get from our loved ones early in life really helps us. I had to celebrate my mother in this piece.

Big Inside

We made fun of the big boy
His belly was large
We thought it was fun
To cry from laughing so hard
That he was embarrassed
to come to school
Or play in the school yard
He even avoided the gate
We only saw him from afar
At the end of the school year
A great lesson we learned
If you laugh at others
It will soon be your turn
He graduated with honours
Earned awards
And great grades
That made us realise
the foolishness of our ways
Maybe something else he had
Was big as well
That brain in his head
The size of his cells
Made us look small
his grades rose, ours fell
He went on to do great things
He always excelled

It's never good to have a good time at someone else's expense. At best others should benefit from the joy we experience. But growing up this was often not the case. I and many of my friends had the common habit of making fun of others in an attempt to feel better about ourselves. People are all different. Those differences make us valuable in different ways. As children, some of my peer group often felt physical difference was an opportunity to belittle others. But we later learned that what we thought people lacked in one area of life they might have an abundance of in other areas. And this was the case with one of the young people we grew up with.

Prints Charming

Who is the king
Can you tell by his clothes
Who is the queen
Can you tell by her robe
In the animal kingdom
Who belongs on the throne
If we judge by how they're dressed
We could all get it wrong

Some say it's the lion
But compared to the cheetah
I'm not quite sure
Standing next to the zebra

They run rings around candidates
But can't dance like the lemur
And the leopard is regal
always spotted
like Saturday night fever

The nature of royals
Colour codes for the spoils
Who can out do
The coral snake
when they're coiled

If we head to the sea
And look at the whale shark
The octopus & cuttle-fish
Who can change colours
Light up in dark
It's hard to chose
They all make their mark
Even without paint brushes
They display beautiful art

So is it the best dressed
Or who has the best teeth
Who works together to survive
With the best hunting techniques

I love how they all look
The peacock and the parrot
The Orca's two tones
Should never feel embarrassed
They remind me of the piano
And music we cherish
So who would you say
Is the most regal
And the most proud
Who should be awarded
This glorious crown

I love design and nature. So I find it fascinating how nature is so beautifully designed. I also love fashion and how it influences the world. This piece acknowledges the ongoing relationship between appearance and status. Not that clothes or appearance determine our worth. But naturally clothes or appearance do allow us to express our uniqueness in amazing ways. In human nature fashion or clothing can create, suggest, or acknowledge passions, levels of status or symbols in society. But that applies variously different in the animal kingdom where the lions are known as the kings, in spite of their plain appearance compared to some of the more elaborately 'clothed' animals.

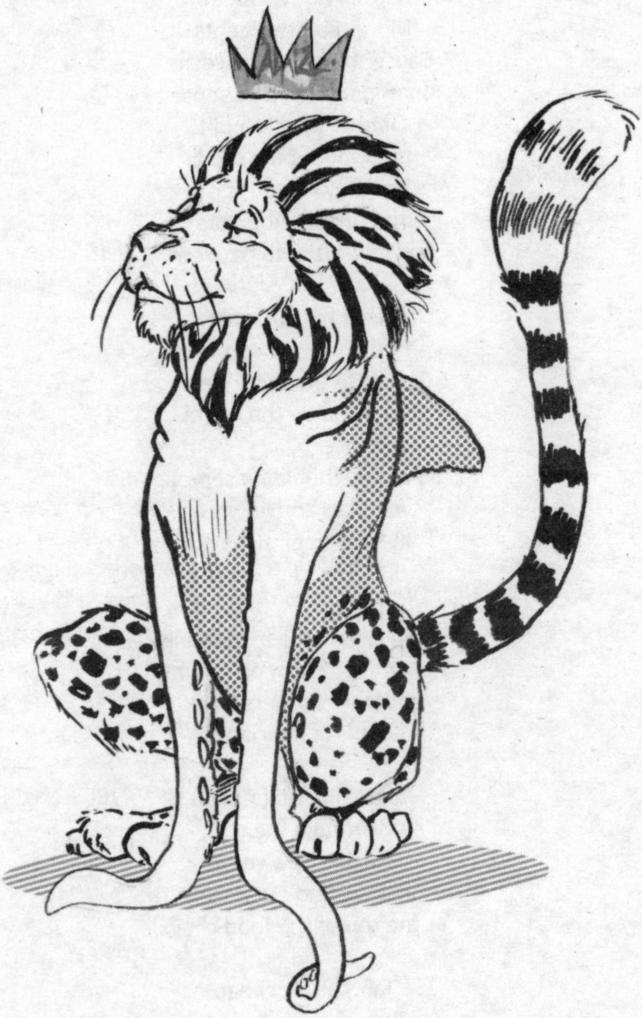

Lip Service

Lip service is worth
More than two cents
Cause the tone of a voice
Gives people a true sense
Of how they're built
their inner blue print
so they can design
and own their house
And love work to pay rent

See words are water
in the form of sound
that rinse the mind clean
and resource the towel

So words should be served
As verbs and vowels
That keep beef moving by
like a herd of cows

With words one can exchange
new thoughts for old brains
til the way others think
travels in new lanes

til the life that flows
through them
creates new veins
and we find ourselves
at the top of the food chain

Talk can be cheap
But when it's sense
that's less common
It all adds up
To help solve any problem

Our lips serve a purpose. And I find that mine are most useful for sharing encouragement and knowledge through performance. Speaking is one of our greatest resources for learning. Much of what we learn is from speaking with others. That being true it's best that we learn how to use our lips to their greatest capacity.

Class Bloom

Don't be fooled
This is a jewel
Being a student is cool
Some of life's best lessons
Are learned following rules
you may think
being kept in class
while times pass is quite cruel
but where would you rather be
doing what in what room

If this room were a car
To where would you drive it
Where would you go
To discover treasure
On your own island

School is the tool
That helps you do the mileage
It's the vehicle
That moves you through
Until you find it

In school you're surrounded
By brilliance and passion
Energy that works like chemistry
In your classes
Even when there's differences
Debates and clashes
It's sharpening your ability
For questions and asking

The classroom is the soil
The brain is a seed
In the right environment
You can harvest a dream

But without the right tools
You'll leave school in need
So the fact is
We need school indeed

See knowledge is power
But you gotta stay plugged in
If not when you flip the switch
You'll still be struggling
To see or make a difference
It will be puzzling
The big picture in pieces
You're left juggling
But when it all comes together

You'll harvest in any weather
Education makes us grow
in shorts, coats or sweaters

The roots of education are bitter, but the fruit is sweet. – Aristotle

Education is the passport to the future, for tomorrow belongs to those who prepare for it today. – Malcolm X

An investment in knowledge pays the best interest. – Benjamin Franklin

There was a time in my life when I thought I hated school. I enjoyed the fact that my friends were there. But I just felt like I couldn't understand how the information being taught would affect my life. I eventually learned that school and education are about connecting with our interests in life. This helped me see school differently. As young people we usually have the first fourteen years of our lives to figure out our interests. However depending on what we're exposed to, we can actually know our interests from as young as five to seven years old. When we become aware of this it opens the world to us in an entirely new way. We start to see connections to aspects of the world and ourselves that makes us love being alive. We should all love life. And education is the tool that helps that love deepen daily. School is very cool. Learning is fun. I heard someone say once 'When we learn we earn'. When we're learning we're growing.

Face My Fears

You could read my face
with your hands
when I hit my teens
I would've used sand paper
If it could have scrubbed it cleaned
Grind down my skin
til it was smooth again
I hadn't invited it
it just started moving in
first it was my chin
next it was my cheeks
facing the mirror in the morning
made me want to stay home for weeks
why is this happening to me
what did I do
to have to wear this mask
everyday to school
this wasn't me
I wanted my old self back
But I want to grow up
I told my old self that
But now that I'm here
I want my growth held back
But then I saw friends
face the same impact
And I learned to face the fact
this was just a phase in life
that it would soon pass
like the day turns to night
and I had peace again
from some amazing advice
you won't be young forever
Learn to embrace change
it's nice

Growing pains come in all shapes and sizes over many issues in life. The arrival of acne on my face in my teenage years was initially a major one for me. So much so that in trying to remove a mistaken one I aggravated a chicken pock that had just started to appear. My attempt increased the spread of chicken pox over my body and led to me missing the school wide sports day on the last day of school. I was beyond disappointed. But I'm so thankful for my mother who encouraged me greatly and took good care of me. It took me a while to grow in patience during those years as appearance seemed to mean so much. Eventually my patience did develop as well as my maturity about appearance and not being so overwhelmed about physical appearance. It's a common experience and I had more peace when I saw others I knew going through it as well.

CURRENCY

The world is your oyster
It's best you learn to swim
Navigate the tides of change
Cause a wave could be your best friend
Carrying you along
When your energy wears thin
Until you both reach the deepest point
Of the destination
The point where you dive
Beneath the surface of time
To discover a shell
With your pearl trapped inside
The jewel once hidden
But now revealed as your greatest pride
That will fund your adventures
On travels worldwide
It is passion that connects
To the growing depths of life
Once found
It fills lungs & gives the best advice
The needed directions forward, backwards
lefts and rights
Even when detours interrupt as oil spills or building sites
Passion is the pull that helps draw up plans
To build dreams in deserts to a tall expanse
Though to others
it might seem a fantasy
with no chance
but to the dreamer
it is an Atlantis at first glance

If time is money we should invest it in dreams. Dreams and goals carry us further than anyone can foresee. In fact our achieved dreams generally out live us. I think about Johannes Gutenberg or Neil

Armstrong. Without them the printing press or man's first visit to the moon wouldn't exist. Johannes made reading text, and educating ourselves through printed books, accessible to all people. I believe dreams and goals hold our worth in this world, that what we value is valuable to others and helps us connect with them. Just think about it. Most of our friends or people we speak to the most have common goals and dreams and that is generally why we value them as much as we do.

Memory Lane

My memory lane
has no yellow bricks
No lion, tin man, Dorothy, or scare crow
But it does have sticks
sharp pricks plus stones
Words as hard as pebbles
that settled as seeds whenever thrown
on the path that I would travel
to destination from the door of home
weeds sprang up that cluttered
and made rough
whenever they were sown
Almost completely hiding a travel route
When they were fully grown
your nose is too big
you're too slow
your clothes aren't very nice
but I was driven by an inward vision
so when I came to lefts and rights
forks interrupting my road
it was then different paths I chose
Often challenging
many times isolated
I felt alone
I'd use this vision as shears
to clean my path and focus my eyes
to see my destination clear
Alone I learned
Lanes aren't wide or large
but often quite narrow
which takes less time
to hit my bullseye
Moving swift as an arrow
My goals guided me
Through murky times

Silently
I'd reflect on moments past
Seeing where others got stuck
lost control at their will
Then eventually they would crash

People can be unpleasant at times for attention. And it's so easy to become a follower when it appears things are fun or popular. But I learned very early in life that not everything that's popular is fun, and that not everything that's fun is popular. So I began to make decisions that insured I'd have great experiences that didn't put me or other people in harms way. That became my lane. It's not always easy to be different. But when it's for the right reasons it is rewarding when you see the benefits.

Caught In The Brain Storm

A rare moment captured
can catapult the captive
to heights of heroes
and skyscraper stature
when our minds
are combined with intrigue and laughter
it's a chemistry lesson
with limitless benefactors
at the speed of light
chains can break
keys release locks
to once forbidden gates
when words go flash
when words go quake
look out for the brain storm
when words take shape
at a moments notice
the impact's explosive
from zero to sixty
here comes a locomotive
a train of thought can leap out
into an ocean
arriving at city gates
that have never been opened
clouds form above
currents form below
anticipation rising
for the biggest show
ideas coming to life
from the depths of one's soul
one brain storm
can change an entire globe

It is amazing how small moments or occurrences in life over time have the biggest effect. It's like the ripple of one drop in a body of water that happens so many times til waves are created. This happens with thoughts as well. Isaac Newton is a great example. When he saw an apple fall from a tree, he wondered why it didn't fall in a different direction other than straight down. This prompted his curiosity and soon after he came up with the idea of the law of gravity. I believe these types of moments happen everyday in our minds and many of them go unnoticed maybe due to busyness. But if we capture those moments of curiosity I believe they have the potential to make a significant difference in our lives if we research and build upon them. So everyday I now record little voice notes in my phone of as many of my curiosities and creative ideas that I have daily. It could be ideas for poems, songs, artwork, photography, plays, books, clothing designs, sports, community projects, any inspiring thoughts that come to me. I think of it as an ideas bank. So when I come back to any of those ideas and begin to ponder them they can grow into something so amazing that my creativity stirs and gets ready to make an impact like a storm.

Steam

A low self esteem
Can make you an air head
So when I have nightmares
I put those to bed

trying to live up to expectations
can push you off the edge
So instead of giving up
I'd rather push the lead

Go push the envelope with words
to deliver royal mail
addressed to the world
like oil for sell
coal under the crucible
with a boiling smell
cause I'm not afraid of the fire
that purifies my cells

see the heat is in kitchen
and so is the food
So when the pressure goes up
You gotta keep your cool
there's dishes being prepared
In your heart to feed a room

Don't let the steam
Go to your head
Just let it
Detox you of doom

Most times when I write I have ideas in concepts. This one came to me as a comparison between our self confidence or self esteem and actually steam we see during cooking. I find it interesting that both rise and fall. Just like water boils then turns to steam and rises from a pot, life can become hot or challenging for us as well and cause us to rise in anger, doubt, or confidence that we can rise to any challenge. I've learned to see challenges as opportunities to exceed my limitations and grow. Seeing life this way makes everyday awesome and empowering.

Roots To The Sky

I've learned to
Feed dreams
And starve nightmares
So I'm often up late
Spending time in the night air
studying to take flight
Like athletes in Nike airs
the Co-pilot in cockpits
In leather seats and nice chairs
Aviation has become
something I greatly admire
whoever knew
gravity was to encourage our defiance
there are natural laws that exist
but there is also a hidden science
Waiting for us to discover
master and apply it
When it happened to me
I felt fleet on my feet
When I learned how to
scale great heights
through words & speech
I learned how to write
And gained rights to new strength
When I often felt in life
Very small, timid, and weak
A geek I became
A nerd in every sense a book worm
digging into pages
Finding my roots in every turn
Fruit ripe so firm
Nothing rotten no germs
My words grew wings
The jet stream I learned

I took a bite and felt weightless
So when I write I feel any weight shift
Any pressure on me
I'm able to escape it
I've found what I love
And my reasons why
The fruits of my labour
Connect me to the sky

Many years ago humanity was limited by gravity. However over time through science and creativity we've learned to overcome gravity in some ways. So I am constantly amazed at how we have learned to defy or work the laws of gravity. The process of writing makes me feel the same amazement. Coming up with imaginative concepts that share ideas in creative ways with people is so fun to me. Words are also limitless in their ability to travel. Once we learn to love and master writing there's nowhere in the world we can't go.

Food For Thought

If I had known then what I know now
I would have read thousands of books
Set my mind down at the table
of authors who learned to cook
Who satisfied their own appetites to know
Through research and development
to have known that then I would have seen
The main ingredients of my own intelligence

How questions are the answers
Curiosity cooks the cake
Desires are the flames
That bring out the rich taste

Decades of understanding
in one to six hours of reading
If I had known then what I know now
I would have been greedy
Chapters one to five for breakfast
Six to ten for lunch
Eleven to twenty for dinner
Twenty one to twenty five
For a late night munch

I would have fed my mind more
If I knew it was my greatest muscle
Able to instruct my body to moves weights
And solve life's greatest puzzles

But now that I know
What I didn't know then
I'm creating my own library of food
And a mental exercise gym

Reading is eating for the brain. I didn't thoroughly understand this early in life. Although I did enjoy reading comic books. I didn't necessarily have the idea that not only could I read and learn from others as well as their work it could help me develop my own stories and poems. When I was around twelve years old this did happen to me which I'll talk about in a later poem.

Know It All

Did you ever know
That you didn't know
What others thought you knew
Cause if they did know
You wouldn't know exactly what to do
At times it seems normal
To act like you know
When you haven't got a clue
Your face says it clearly
Though you try to hide it from view

But to know what you don't know
Is really what makes us true
You see know it alls
don't know it all
They just know what they do

When they do what they know
They stand out from the crowd
Though what they know can be small
Its sound can be loud

So when you know what you know
You should acknowledge it proud
And stand on it
through all of life's ups and downs

Stand on what you know
Til what you know is in demand
Cause what you know
Will always give you a set of powerful hands
To find out what you need to know
And make your knowledge expand

> So acknowledge what you don't know
> And start documenting a plan
> And don't let others stir you wrong
> Just be driven to understand

I used to get nervous when around or in groups of people. Sometimes because I felt that most people knew more than me. Now I understand that people do know more than me in different subjects. And I know more than others in different subjects. No one knows everything about everything. So we should never feel inadequate regardless of who we are around. And it's not how much we know that really matters in life. It's how much we know that is useful to others and that's actually being used for the benefit of others. That's real value. That's understanding. If you think about a dictionary how many words do we use from the dictionary in everyday experiences. Sure all the words are amazing. But there are many that are much more used than others because we understand them.

In Pulses

I'm an electrician
I flip switches
And fix glitches
Go into dark rooms
For lights to start flicking
Vital signs twitching
Where parts were thought missing
Cause once I look inside
I pull apart systems
I'm parts driven
Is it the heart or sparks dimming
So I use a sharp art
to infuse hearts with precision
This thing is off beat
Slow pump
The pulse and rhythm
Are not hitting like they should
Just soft ticking
there should be a thump
a boom, a click and a pow
bright and radio active
as a nuclear towel
So I get to work
quickly put tools in the ground
to make people radiant
with beautiful smiles

Quote from an article online about Human Electricity
Everything we do is controlled and enabled by electrical signals running through our bodies. Scientists agree that the human body, at rest, can produce around 100 watts of power on average. This is enough electricity to power up a light bulb. Some humans have the ability to output over 2,000 watts of power, for instance if sprinting. - Julia Layton

Julia Layton "How does the body make electricity — and how does it use it?" 22 September 2008. HowStuffWorks.com. <https://health.howstuffworks.com/human-body/systems/nervous-system/human-body-make-electricity.htm> 7 December 2021

Did you know the human body produces and uses electricity. That was an extraordinary discovery and thought for me.

However as I've grown into writing and performing I've become more aware of the presence or feeling of energy in rooms full of people. We all have probably felt it. But just didn't recognise it as the presence of electricity. Now that I know that I look at every opportunity to write and perform as a way to tap into energy that already exists in a room. Once I tap in, that room can be become a powerhouse of ideas exchanged that can leave everyone present charged up. So in some ways I see myself as an electrician.

BRIDGES

A lullaby sang to us
Each time we crossed the bridge
notes from no human key
Yet carried emotions for us as kids
The expectation of connection to something tangible
Something of worth
from repeat adventures
To other sides of the city
a search
Across a river that separated its population
Downtown from the ghetto
The courthouse from the Capital buildings grassy meadows
Metal objects don't usually sing
Yet we were left to interpret the tune
Its theme
Every journey a new lyric
Our childhood young spirits
looking for directions
to our place in this world
It's amazing how close the ghetto was to the capital
Yet we knew nothing of bills or lobbyist
In the lobbies of shops we sat
Wanting the newest sneakers
And basketball kits
Our hopes of freedom
Expressed on courts across the lengths of
cities, states, and television screens
As I recall there were two bridges
This one was different
It was suspended as I was in every note it carried
Reminded of the deserted house every year
On one side and the Library on the other
The people they said who lived under it
And how we never saw them
And how dangerous the openings of the railings were
As you walked across it

For the majority of my childhood til age 15 I realised I lived in capital cities of states in the US located by major rivers, Trenton, New Jersey and Frankfort, Kentucky, and now London, England. The Delaware river flowed through Trenton, the Kentucky river through Frankfort and the Thames flows through London. So where ever I have lived there have always been bridges around. I didn't realise it then but they were significant to our urban upbringing. My brother and I loved traveling across bridges. They suggested adventure and crossing over potential obstacles to discover new opportunities and experiences. One particular bridge became quite significant to me as I approached my teenage years. It was called the singing bridge in Frankfort, Kentucky. Every time you traveled across it in a car it would make a very unique sound. This sound always reminded me of the emotions I felt at the time in my life.

Glass Ceiling

Someone said
the sky's the limit
But last I checked
It doesn't finish
there's nothing to separate
the sky from space
just our vision
and when the sky grows dark
from earth changing its position
what we see grows as well
when our light source goes missing
how do we see further in the dark
than we do in the light
we see clouds high in the day
but stars higher at night
compared to the moon
stars are further away in height
So does the sky really have limits
I'm not sure that's right

So if the sky doesn't
Do we have any
Throughout history
Mankind has gone beyond many
Does that mean we can grow
Where there's lack have plenty
If we learn to look beyond
Difficulties life gives us, see

If earth's ceiling is made of glass
Are it's walls as well
Are there obstacles in front of us
We've found hard to tell
We see visions in our minds
getting there
Often seems hard as nails

Iron bars and giant guards
Saying these are uncharted trails
But our thoughts find them familiar
Our hearts propelled
Drawn like a magnet
Through the stratus
like kites that sail

It's taken telescopes to tell us folks
There are other planets
Unveiled
what we never knew before
It seems knowledge is a well
A bottomless resource
A deep force with swells
That forks like rivers run
to ports that carry mail
This retorts what some report
Of hopes at shortened scale
So it's the eye of the beholder
That controls the tale

Can we see it now
Our mind has the biggest eyes
If we can imagine it
It can be created and designed
Even glass was an invention
Discovered over time
That over heat you could
Create transparent material
and dishes from lime

So now we're different inside
Let our vision be aligned
With our hopes and dreams
Not restricted to time
Any distance we can rise
Our eyes are free
To look as far as
Our minds can see

Have you ever heard this phrase or figure of speech 'The sky's the limit'? I've never really used it myself. But I have often heard it used to encourage people that possibilities are endless. Recently as I began to think more deeply about this expression it has become more encouraging to me. There does seem to be a limit to sky during the day time when we generally see its blue colour or clouds. However once the earth rotates and the sun goes down as we call it, we begin to actually see beyond the sky into space. This is often possible during the day as well as we see the sun and sometimes the moon. But on a night clear of clouds we are able to see stars that are millions of miles away from earth. So the sky doesn't really have a limit other than our ability to see beyond it, due to the time of day it is. I hope this can encourage people about the limitless possibilities that exist in their lives that only seem visible at different times. If we keep those possibilities in mind and work toward them one day we can reach them just like humanity, through scientists, have figured out how to travel to the moon and now even beyond.

WORDS WORTH

Don't desert me
Because I am a desert see
the cherry on top
when you learn to exert me
I can wet your whistle
whenever you're thirsty
and be spoken so politely
people stop and curtsey
when you learn to work me
I'll work at the worst feat
till it becomes your best
and people say you're worthy
to be called a smith
when you beat me into bits
sharp enough to cut through
any type of myth
because I am the gift
that stays ever present
on whatever you rap me
I solve or explain the question
I can make everything exciting
Keep life interesting
I'm heavy on your hand
I'll always leave an impression
Make it all attractive
the ultimate possession
Of language packaged
That increases in value
the more you practise
You can earn your keep
And be worth more
Than you can imagine
If you find the worth in your words
You'll make infinite transactions

A picture's worth a thousand
Well think of your life time
If you live one hundred years
How much could you write rhymes

I once heard someone say intelligence can be measured by the size of your vocabulary. I do believe that is true in some ways. But not totally based on how many words you know. But how well you know how to use them. As a poet, rapper, songwriter, and musician I know from experience how a creative use of words can help you succeed in life generally and financially. I used to think rapping was cool. But when I learned how to do it my cool points went up and how confident I felt about myself even more so. It was something I wanted to do ever since I first heard it. Learning how to use my own vocabulary to come up with poems and songs really amazed me and still does. When you think about how many ways the same words can be used it's just amazing. And the more words we learn the more combinations we can use. It gets me excited just thinking about it.

Master Key

If you had the key
What door would you unlock
To what room in what house
In what city on what block
In what state in what country
on what continent on whose clock
would you use the hands of time
before the tick stops

Asia, Africa, Europe, North America,
South America, Antarctica, or Australia
what bridge could you build
to cross over failure
and help fulfil the potential
of every youth and every elder

Just think about it
If you had the keys to the city
what change would you arrange
to put in place with your committee
Feed the hungry
Build shelters for the homeless
Run a clothing drive
For those who lack clothing
A key is anything
That can get a door open
It can be a vision or idea
That sets change in motion

I believe every person on earth has a key that unlocks something that others need. So how do we discover the key we have. It starts with our desire to make positive changes in the world. Once we recognise that desire and the abilities and skills we have we can start planning and taking action. If we saw someone walking down the road carrying more bags than they could manage we'd probably want to help them. That desire to help and our physical ability to do so is our key. This is the same with anything else in life. When we are moved emotionally by something that is a trigger to show us we have a desire to help. Then it is our responsibility to figure out how we can help.

Maple Cheeks

The tower of power
The stack brown and golden
Crushed flower
From a powder
A beautiful morning moment

Flat and round
the shape of perfection
the aroma of them cooking
Would wake you from resting
This part of my childhood
left a great impression
this morning cuisine
a great selection

Mother's special touch
my grandmothers as well
the butter they would spread
the cinnamon you could smell

sitting neatly on a plate
growing taller every minute
steam rising from the pan
the excitement sizzling

busy in the kitchen
oven mitts and aprons
building them for us
while we lacked the patience
ready to devour tall towers
we waited
to smother them in maple syrup
and our smiling faces

What do you know about pancakes? If nothing yet I would encourage to get to know about pancakes. Ask your parents or guardian to make some for you. This simple food is one of the things I miss most about America. In fact I think some American foods in general I miss. There's another one we have called the Philly Cheese Steak. Geez...! I'm getting hungry just talking about these. No they're not extremely healthy for you. But their taste is amazing. Pancakes were a favourite of ours growing up. Beautiful golden brown, fluffy, flat, flour cakes we could top with delicious maple syrup, with a tall glass of ice cold milk. We would scrape the plate with our forks to finish every bit. Many of the foods in the US originate from other places. And such is the case with pancakes. I did a bit of research on pancakes and found they may have originated in Greece. The following information cites some references.

https://www.bettycrocker.com/menus-holidays-parties/mhplibrary/seasonal-ideas/the-unofficial-happy-history-of-pancakes

600 BC - The first recorded mention of pancakes dates back to ancient Greece and comes from a poet who described warm pancakes in one of his writings.

1100 AD – Shrove Tuesday (Pancake Day) becomes a traditional way to use up dairy products before Lent – the pancake breakfast is born.

Hope Less

If you've ever felt hopeless
I encourage you
hope less
But do more
then watch your progress
Movement alone
moves you along
And is known to stretch
you into the unknown
right beyond your own stress
into a place of discovery
where life becomes lovely
and things become beautiful
that once seemed ugly
fraught with skull duggery
and lack of a future
cause doing brings energy
surely a booster
I make a checklist
And have that with my breakfast
It's the road map for my day
With dIrections
Tolls and exits
Rest points and methods
To navigate my day
So I don't feel restless
When ever is running low
I just go and catch it

Hope is the expectation of and desire for change. Many times we can feel hopeless if we aren't seeing changes we desire. But I have learned in life that it can be good to do something while we're waiting for other things to change or happen. It may seem weird. But creating change in other areas can take our minds off the other things we're waiting for and give us more energy because we're seeing something change.

Sometimes I do this with writing poems, songs, or playing musical instruments. When learning or creating new work I'll take a break from one of those activities and do the other for a bit. Then when I go back to the other I have a new energy and perspective to add to it.

LEGENDS

Heroes from our city
Never had capes
but got blood on their uniforms
and mud on their face
we only saw them on Friday nights
when their shoe tongues were laced
the sun had gone to sleep
and flood lights lit up the space
our neighbourhoods came to watch
our warriors do battle
in soldier pads and legs clad
running like horses to score and tackle
mists from their mouths
Under the blanket of night
in the winter chill
steaming from their helmets
from the efforts and skill
how sharp they were
you could tell they were drilled

play after play the execution
the power the will
the courage the intensity
of bodies crashing together
or the simplicity
of sprinting down the field
like an olympic scene
made crowds stand to their feet
We roared the biggest of screams
we were captivated by the performance
the impact was enormous
our super heroes didn't have capes
But their presence was transforming
No Batman or Robin
No commissioner Gordon
No Gotham

But whenever they appeared
It was easy to spot em
But they gave us hopes and dreams
That inspired us to learn to solve problems
With natural abilities
In athletics and humility

Sports did and still do have a big influence on my life. As far back as I can remember I've wanted to be an athlete and have played sports. Some of the people I grew up with were some of my greatest heroes. In fact my older brother is among them. When I think of it now I feel quite privileged to have grown up around so many amazing athletes. They inspired me to give my all in athletics in attempts to become a professional American football player. My efforts eventually earned me a scholarship to university where I became a great wide receiver and All American special teams player at Morehead State University.

Superman, Spiderman, X men and all the others are amazing characters created out of the imagination of some amazingly creative people. But there are superheroes in our daily lives as well that inspire us to do our best and overcome obstacles to achieve our goals and dreams. This is a tribute to the inspirations who inspired me to fulfil my greatest potential. Without a cape or mask they were and are still superheroes in my eyes.

TEXT YOURS

Words rest on our flesh
Our feelings on sleeves worn
Verbal cotton
audio linen
Some are sharp as thorns
Covering our bodies
When expressed they adorn
Who we are
And what we become
From the day we are born

They prick parts unseen
Leaving internal piercings
That hang on earlobes
Longer than gold earrings

They are felt
They are fabric
They clothe our mind
They can be plain
be lavish
Create inner pictures designed
They are wool when pulled
They can cover the eyes
And leave things unseen
And others disguised

They can be taught to the heart
And to a parent's surprise
To hear their child
Speak the language
Of love from their tribe

So when I write
I acknowledge the feeling
is it soft is it rough

Does it leave skin peeling
Does it cause a squirm
A tug
Or a twitch

A grimace on the face
From an irritating itch
Or do people smile
Or radiant
Whenever they catch a glimpse
Of how they feel
From what comes from my lips

These are the measures I take
From crown to footprint
How words have made me feel
I've developed a good sense
Of how to address others
In a way that I desire
Words are a second skin
A glorious attire

I believe words have texture much like the clothes we wear. I believe they actually affect us more than what we wear. When I've researched influential people and their lifestyles I've found that many actually value the power of the words much greater than anything else. So I wanted to share that in this piece. This poem is also reflective of my experiences as a performer and in conversation. You discover how words are received. They really do rest on us like clothing and cause us to feel deeply.

WRITERS BLOCK

Ready or not
You best get ready to jot
cause when you were born
there was the setting of a clock
the time your life would span
like the measure of a lot
to find your hidden talents
like treasure under plots
So out the gate
when alarms ring you from sleep
jump out of bed
like a rabbit on its feet
hop to it in your heat
But stay in your lane
life's a relay
gotta run your race
before the exchange
you gotta stride it out
set the pace
Focus on the glory through pain
because history is a podium
that wants to hang metals
on your name

So block out bits of time
to reflect on what you've done
where you fell short
and where you were number one
when the crowd cheered you on
where your emotions felt numb
when your heart was in your mouth
still beating like a drum
then you learned the rhythm
and you kept the pulse

> you channelled the energy
> like metal carries volts
> conducting the charge
> and a symphony of voices
> in a hall of fame of hope
> exhibiting a champions choices

Sometimes as a writer a blank page can be intimidating. What should I write? Will anyone like it? Can I communicate my idea clearly? Will they appreciate my ideas? There can be so many questions that make us question our creative ability. But if we look back on our lives we'll see that we've always been creative in one way or another. Everybody on earth is creative in some way. So when we recognise that and previous moments of creativity, we can use those as blocks of inspiration to build from for our process of creative writing. In many athletics events blocks are used as supports for competitors to push off of with their feet to get the race started. That is the idea I was going for here. Looking at small moments of creativity in our lives that we can push off of to start on new ones. Discovering our own voice through creative writing is so liberating and empowering. Imagine the world waiting to hear what you have to say about life, you sharing it, then one, tens, hundreds or even thousands of different people standing in ovation for the brilliance you've shared. It can happen. It's happened to me.

Charlie Brown

He was a man's best friend
we were just little boys
the two tones of his curly hair
brought us so much joy
walks by the river
that we swam in too
squeezed his longs ears
he'd lick us
tongue part blue
so playful so intelligent
a protector and affectionate
he made everyday fun
we threw things
he'd go fetching it

his brown and white coat
kept us warm in the cold
during the winter
we threw balls
played in the snow

on the leash or not
at parks or our apartment blocks
he obeyed our every word
even when we didn't say a lot

He could read our face
would jump in our laps
curl up and rest his head
waiting for the rub of his back
fall asleep on us
make us so relaxed

When we moved
it broke our hearts
I think I still feel the cracks

If dogs could talk I bet they would say some amazing things. They have such a great ability to make us feel loved. We had several dogs over our years growing up. But Charlie Brown our Cocker Spaniel was surely our favourite. It's amazing how you can love an animal like you would a person. Or at least we did. I remember shedding tears when we had to give Charlie Brown away when we moved from New Jersey to Kentucky in the United States. I know full well why they say a dog is a man's best friend.

Eye See You

Mirrors are all around us
Not just on walls
Some walk around
Some stand in halls
Some talk back to us
Some just look and listen
But one thing they all do
Is reflect our condition
Our inner position
Our thoughts
And what we share
And the clearest ones
Are really sharp
Best kept near
As we age in life
And time goes by
Who we really are
They help us identify
How do you recognise a mirror
It's usually when it recognises you
And confirms something about yourself
That you already knew
But from a different angle
A more interesting view
Subtle differences limitless
Over time that become new
Family, friends, or even strangers
Have the ability to contribute
And change us
With a word or
Just a look has a language

The most valuable people in our lives are the ones who see and value us for who we are and appreciate our vision of the future. At least once a day I would say everyone looks into a mirror. Why do we do this? We want to see ourselves, and if the physical person matches the thoughts we have of ourselves. This same action happens with our families, friends, and even strangers. We look at or communicate with people with the expectation that their response to us will confirm our thoughts of ourselves. It's an amazing relationship to recognise.

HEIR BORN

Good evening captains & cadets
Are you prepared to fly your jet
Are your instruments calibrated
Have you even checked
the flight path for your arrival
have coordinates been set
You can't even leave the ground
if your course is not correct

See you were born to fly
cause time does without planning
It will pass you by
leave you on the runway standing
If you don't get in the jet-stream
and develop understanding
that you can be carried along
by momentum already on the planet

there's pathways to paradise
carriage ways in the clouds
maybe not rainbow coloured
but the spectrum is wow

when you see what others have done
through what history has written down
combined with your inner visions
what could exist right now

you'll have a ticket and a diploma
to travel to every corner
earth has to offer
or even further

They've now landed on the moon
and taken pictures of Mars
So if you aim for the clouds
You will land amongst stars

Knowing history gives us inspiration for the future. If we know what others have achieved it gives us a sense of what we are capable of. I've often heard people say we stand on the shoulders of giants. Meaning others accomplishments will be the foundations of ours. When I first heard the poet Saul Williams in the film Slam he put my imagination on the runway of creativity. Then the rappers Mos Def, Nas, Ghostface from Wu Tang Clan, Rakim, Black Thought, LL Cool J, and Common caused me to take off. It happens with everyone when we plug into the energy that is already active on the Earth. Did you know that scientists say the amount of energy on Earth never changes. It's always the same amount. If that's the case the difference is who taps into the energy or not. When you discover you have a love for something if you research those who've excelled at that same passion before you and others who are excelling now you'll find an energy and inspiration source that will help you achieve your dreams.

SPEECHLESS

As the cushion
Of our youth wore thin
Foul words invaded my mouth
The force of a falling anvil
Crushing my heavy heart
Known to all but my parents
Home had rules
Though broken
Though growing more wayward
I managed still to respect my mother
Confused by the pain in my language
My emotions a wall less prison
In which I served a sentence
unwritten it seemed
You're not allowed to say what you feel
Until you come of age
At what number would that be
When would I be free
To know what freedom is
when shackles become foreign
For lips sealed by morning
Fruitless seeds starved
Before they were ever sown
I was born with a tongue
I couldn't sharpen
Because if I did someone would get hurt
Yet there was thirst
To share this pain
At least one drop

The validity of young people's perspectives can often be dismissed or disregarded. This is not healthy for the present or the future. It can make being young very challenging. Considering that young people are the future of society it is very important that young voices are heard and supported in a way that nurtures their greatest qualities. During our process of maturing into adults we begin to develop our own opinions and perspectives. It seems quite natural that people should expect a fresh view on the familiar when a person has new experiences. These perspectives are what push society forward to new capacities. The Wright Brothers thought they could create a vehicle that could fly people around the world. They were initially dismissed. Today people fly all across the world everyday of the week.

Free Air

What we most depend on
We can't even see
it can't be held in our hand
and the cost is free
it's amazing
when you think about it cautiously
and makes you appreciate
the awesome trees
but if it did cost
how would you price it
who could sell it
how would they get a licence
Could you buy it in public
Or only in private
It makes you realise
Its value is priceless

It's odd to ask
But if we did have to pay
For the oxygen we breathe
By the hour or day
Could everyone afford it
Some not some may
According to where they live
And play

Our relationship to trees
How we treat the earth
Shows how we measure
its value and worth

There are more trees in certain countries
Would they pay less
And charge other countries more
For air that's fresh

South America would probably be first
With its Amazon rainforest
The Congo in Africa
Would be the second most important

How would this affect the world
If it wasn't free
What we need the most
But can't even see

The health of our planet earth has become a hot topic recently. Many are very concerned about climate control and change for good reason. Due to some mismanagement of Earth's resources its natural beauty and balance are being damaged. Some animals face unnecessary extinction. Some oceans have unhealthy coral and fish populations. The uncommon temperature change in colder regions is causing potentially dangerous increased water levels and the loss of habitat for animals that live there. How we treat Earth is so important. It's so easy to take things for granted that are seemingly free, until we realise how valuable they are.

Bubble Guts

Shoosh
be quiet keep your head low
if you don't acknowledge it
no one will know
no one will ask
and no one will tell
if you don't say anything
they won't notice the smell
just look the other way
act like you're busy
and don't breathe it in
you might get dizzy
don't look forward
let anyone catch your eyes
an eyebrow flinch could be your demise
if the elevator is full
or the room has one person there
just act normal
as if you're breathing fresh air
just give it a moment
the aroma
It will pass
hopefully a breeze will come
to remove it fast
But don't change your expression
remain calm it's a must
or it will be obvious
you're guilty
of having the bubble guts
Bubble guts
What's that
did I hear someone ask
If you had bubbles in your guts
Wouldn't you be full of gas
And if somebody slapped your shoulder
Wouldn't you let out a huge blast

And wouldn't they look at you funny
And cause other people to gasp
Yes that's why
You must strive to keep a secret
Everyone gets the bubble guts
from certain foods
We just have to learn
To be discreet with it

This has happened to me on several occasions, or I've been where it's happened on several occasions. And it's always a bit weird because you can instantly become a detective trying to figure out who's committed this crime. There you are in a public space minding your own business and bam it hits you right in the nose. So what do you say? What do you do? Do you look around. Usually I don't. But I have often wondered if anyone would be brave enough to say, 'Hey that was me. I did that. My apologies. It was something I ate.' But if they did I wonder how people would react. Would they consider it polite that the person admitted to it. I'm not sure. But it surely happens to all of us as our bodies react to the foods we eat. But it's surely best to try to be discreet away from others.

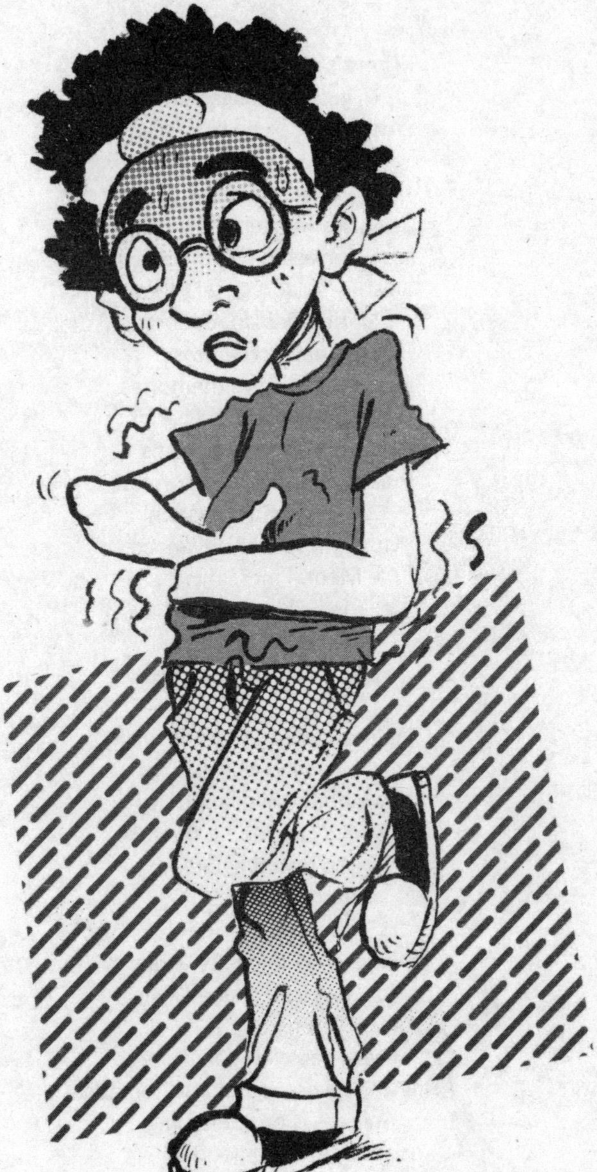

Habit To Grab It

There's a secret to success
to getting things done
Anything can be mastered
Activity under the sun
Time is a factor
But to shorten the sum
If we invest in this practice
Destiny's package will come
Our bodies' functions
All have programs
Our muscles have memories
That direct and hold hands
Our brains have systems
That deliver like the postman
But it's a better system
Much more well advanced
Mental messaging
invisible memos
When we get hot
We look to open windows

We learn to eat, talk and walk
but once we have
we don't think about it
our brains just repeat the tasks
So just imagine
If this was something
people applied
To what they'd love to achieve
How it would change lives

Every day would be a joy
Achieving goals would be automatic
Success is programming
It's the result of good habits

I used to think it was so hard to play musical instruments. In fact I doubted if I could learn how to play any. Then one day I just decided I would find a way to learn. I found some teaching videos and I heard one of the instructors say this may be challenging and take you some time. But take it slowly and if you need to practise one small thing 100 times, do that. Play one chord 100 times on the piano. Even after being an athlete for years, knowing that practice makes perfect, doing something 100 times was a foreign concept to me. But I did it. And what I discovered is that like with most things we do, our muscles have memory. Muscle memory. That may sound strange. But the more you do something your body and muscles actually remember how to do it. Then eventually your body becomes programmed to do it without you even thinking about it. This literally applies to everything we do. If we think about walking, talking, or brushing our teeth, these are all learned actions that now we probably do without even thinking about them. Success just like this is a habit. The more we do something. The easier it becomes.

Head In The Clouds

Times have really changed
I can tell you why
There's a library in the air
A school in the sky
Years ago
We could only afford
to learn from books in buildings
using chalk on boards
But now
it's touch screens and apps
e and audio books
Sat nav no maps
Satellites can show you pictures
of where you live at
We can hold knowledge in our hands
Access billions of facts
You can still check out a book
but it's quicker to download
Read news from every where
the front page all over the globe
Libraries in city centres
Have moved into our homes
the school is where ever we want it
The school is in our phones
We can learn from a distance
at fingertips in an instant
have a new classmate
build a new friendship
Once we left home
to master syllables, sentences, and vowels
But now
We do it
with our head in the clouds

CPUs, gigabytes, and ram
Broadband, wifi, Instagram
Tik Tok, YouTube, with our Facebook fam
Where my Tweebles at
Wave your digital hands

Our heads are in the clouds
We can see for miles
I'm about to live stream
And make my fans all smile
Then afterwards
they can download the show
As a file
And remix some tracks
With others I compile

You can be on top of the world
From the bottom of the earth
Viewed by millions
At home putting in work

The computer and internet have changed the world. There probably hasn't been a time in history when people have been as globally connected as now. It's very exciting and can sometimes be overwhelming trying to keep up with all the new technology we currently use. But when we embrace it properly it seems the opportunities are endless. I remember when only a few people had mobile phones and they came and stayed in bags. Now I don't even have a land line at home. I only use my mobile phone. It's such an amazing transition. It shows you how creative humanity is. When we learn to harness our imagination the possibilities seem limitless.

Hair Dues

You could fade it or wave it
in my hood become famous
from the way you wore your hair
high top or shaved it
Afro picked out
a box cut or braided
if it were going out of style
you had to quickly update it

use wax to control naps
keep it cut on the regular
big designs and hairlines
correct like they had editors
whatever your head size
your cut had to measure up
or get laughed to pieces
or bank status like a trust

There were do's and don'ts
quiet responses or loud jokes
you were guaranteed reactions
from known and foreign folks

You couldn't get by on the sly
Jaws would drop
Laugh you to the bottom
For not keeping a nice top

Girls or boys
no matter the gender
If you had a carrot top
They'd put you in the blender
You had to come correct
Stay fresh and stand your ground
When you did you'd get respect
Like royalty in their crowns

Awarded a cap and gown
cause you graduated
Found a hair patch of the promised land
From stylistic navigation
Proved that you invested time and
That you were patient
Now you're considered a veteran
Even a patron
Or alumni
The birds on the block
Would say you were young and fly
Just a few years back
They would say young'n Why

You got a mop top
Pillow mess, a bed head
Your nickname for the day
Your hair is dread
But not like a rasta's
Nice style and locked up
They'd be like
Who let you leave home
You needed your top cut
But you could be a top cat
With a fresh due
In your cap
Or braided up
Decorated with beads and plaits

Hair style and maintenance were hugely significant to us. Probably in the top five most important list. Food, clothing, shelter, something else, and hair. Nah just kidding. But it was very important. I think for everyone hairstyle is important as it helps establish our identity. I've always loved the creativity of hair. There's so many different styles you can create. We had long hair, short hair, lined designs. I even had dread locks for a while. It has always been fun and you could look nice in whatever clothing that would complement that look. If you look throughout history hair has always been significant in all cultures around the world. It will certainly always be.

Chasing The Wind

Verse 1
Day in and day out
it seems I can't put this flame out
I've got the same taste in my mouth
and it could burn down my whole house
is what I'm told by loved ones who care
but have their own doubts
In wisdom they counsel me to be responsible
I hear them
but following is not probable
inside of me there's desire that rages
And it seems people's words often become cages
I hear keys jingling locked inside their cadence
my natural instincts feel like they're trying to tame it
I'm fearful as if hunted by their statements
is this real or just my imagination
going wild and crazy trying to get the best of me
but when they're full on words I still remain hungry
something's missing
I don't belong here
the only time I feel free
is when I look up in the air

Over the hills and through the woods and through the trees
I'm feeling like foreign goods somewhere overseas
on a chase somehow I move like the breeze
weightless without chains or binds finally free

Verse 2
Every morning I arise
I feel I belong in the sky
seeing life through birds eyes
If no one else believes
I'll teach myself to fly

there's wings on my mind
that my body can't supply
at times I feel immortal
My body's here my mind has escaped
gravity that keeps things on earth's face
there's no weight I feel light as a feather
there's no distance or height my mind couldn't measure
is this natural feeling these types of pleasures
A butterfly sensation as I lift off
my body and soul becoming one with my thoughts
I'm now parallel to the ground I was walking on
I start feeling like those stories about the Parthenon
is this a myth I'm not from Rome
but the more I think
The further I get from home
I hope they won't miss me
Will they realise I'm gone

Over the hills and through the woods and through the trees
I'm feeling like foreign goods somewhere overseas
on a chase somehow I move like the breeze
weightless without chains or binds finally free

Verse 3
Around the world in 80 days or less
I've now learnt to conquer the ruler
That chains all flesh
every day is a new adventure from London to Budapest
France, Jamaica, Germany, Australia
Aruba, the Bahamas, Barbados, Brazil
Chile, Mexico, then Japan
China, the Philippines, Malaysia, Sudan
Egypt, Saudi Arabia, then Iran
Ethiopia, Nigeria, then Morocco
the Ivory Coast, Ghana, Niger, the Congo

I'll be a bongo to celebrate what I've become
in spite of people saying hold your tongue
till I was blue in the face
my body became numb
I'm now at a banquet
I was raised on crumbs
I knew this day would come
I felt it in my gut
the freedom we all crave
but eventually go nuts
I'm out

Over the hills and through the woods and through the trees
I'm feeling like foreign goods somewhere overseas
on a chase somehow I move like the breeze
weightless without chains or binds finally free

These are lyrics from one of my favourite songs that I've ever written. It came from an idea I had of someone chasing a dream so much til they became like the wind where nothing could stop them. It also comes from another saying I heard growing up, 'Chasing a dream is like chasing the wind'. That basically meant that the dream was impossible to catch. That can be a pretty discouraging thing to hear when you're a dreamer. So I realised that I had a reoccurring desire to be a musician and songwriter that would never leave me, regardless if anyone encouraged me to pursue it or not. And some discouraged it. So I decided to pursue my dream which has gotten me to where I am today, as a writer, performer, and musician. In this piece I compare desire to fire and taste, because we often desire to taste something through physical hunger as well as desire to experience some things through dreams and ambitions. So 'Chasing The Wind' is all about my experience with pursuing dreams and how determination can enable you to have experiences you dream about and that others wished they could. I think dreams and ambitions are some of the most important aspects of life. We all need hopes and dreams. They make life beautiful and fun.

STREET ENGLISH

Verse 1
Now this ain't Verona
But it's just as poetic
As watching the Montagues and Capulets going at it
The return of the drums
with narrative street poetry
A play on words
that would make Shakespeare notice me
You could call it Floetry
I'm living in London
Strictly underground
where inspiration is abundant
Big Ben in the back drop
and estates lacking cash crops
where street rats need cheese
and keep the lab hot
from dust til dawn
during midsummers nights
rewriting our stories
without the quills or candlelight
if your literary voice is sharp and handle nice
in a your short amount of time
your grammar could fetch a price
turn a hard-knocks life
into a valiant street merchant
Crown a prince in the ghetto
once seen worthless
a sign for certain
so I hope you get the picture
It's Street English
from curbs we pen scriptures

Verse 2
So consider this
a love letter to rekindle the flame
of a passing vigil
they say is crippled and lame
in a morgue waiting on a head stone and a grave
commemorative plaques for rap
Bearing hip hop's name
Name another genre's
that's been scrutinised the same
For raising cain
minus the same level of blame
So we salute the aims
of our abandoned authors
Raised in poverty
and become world renowned scholars
Masters of communication
and vocal presentations
Til Japanese and Swedish people
learned a new language
Brazilians and Haitians
Czech Republican patrons
All pledging allegiance
to this one nation
One people under hope
Hungry to see freedom
Rooted in a new culture
Repping an old kingdom
A unified voice
A caged bird once wingless
Who learned to take flight
By speaking that street English

I call hip hop music Street English because I believe it is the language of common street people written and spoken in a poetic way that properly depicts the beauty in the struggles of life. I believe this so much that I wrote and entitled an entire rap album after it. This song and these lyrics communicate why I see it that way. I believe Hip Hop culture has unified generations of foreigners globally in a way that nothing else before it has. You can travel to anywhere in the world and hear hip hop music and see Graffiti on walls and see hip hop lifestyles. This is evidence of its global influence and significance. I didn't know it when I started out. But now I can go anywhere in the world as a hip hop artist and feel right at home.

Evolution

Constellations craters orbits axis
there's gravity on earth
outside it
it's absent
When we think about creation
it should cause a reaction
that stirs our minds
keeps our imaginations active
just think about magnets
push and pull
natural attractions
that earth is full
of metal
but also plants organic
there's so much to grasp
from the strength of ants
to other planets
It's so exciting to learn
each day is a new canvas

Everyday like the planets in our solar system we have an opportunity to evolve, to grow. It actually happens whether we want it to or not. As others cause the world around us to change our bodies change to accommodate that and survive. But if we actively engage in the process of learning and growing the outcomes can be amazing. We will grow, we will naturally evolve.

PRESCRIPTION

Dr Seuss was the first doctor
I met
Who taught me how to prescribe medicine
No stethoscope or vest
Til then
I thought medicine came in bottles
Or packaged as pills
But what I read on those pages
Later affected how I'd feel
I laughed on my own
In corners of libraries
having a chuckle
While some kids I knew
Got into all sorts of trouble
The medicine I needed
I didn't find at the chemist
I found it mixing words
That healed me beyond limits
That helped me find an image
I could live up to
Instead of wearing a mask
An unrecognisable reflection
Of how I'd become who
I never imagined or others often became
Because they never found the dose they needed
To alleviate their pain

I heard a quote that a joyful heart is good medicine. I learned this personally when I developed a love for checking out books at our local library and laughing at the content. I think our mother took us there a couple of times as a family first. After that I started to go all the time on my own. I couldn't believe you could have access to all those books for free with just a card. So I would go there and take a stack of books off the shelves, go sit in the corner and read on my own. The first books

I looked for were Dr. Seuss books about this Cat In A Hat that my school teachers had shared in class. It was so fun to discover there were so many different Dr. Seuss books that I'd never heard of. Those books were funny, silly, imaginative, and easy to read. They also had a lot of rhythm and rhyme. It was paradise, rhyming and laughing.

APPLES

I saw him again
For the very first time
A joy that exceeded
any measure of mine
The apple had made it
Back to the tree
Roots no stem
Still connected like string
Traits the same
Features, expressions
Sun and moon
a great reflection
The dawn a new
And the sun setting
Linked only by seed
And growth's natural progression

I love my dad very much. And there was a time in my life when we were separated from each other. When we were reunited it seemed that our love had increased. I remember when we saw each other again for the first time. I had a pair of my favourite sunglasses hanging from my shirt against my chest. He hugged me so tightly my glasses shattered between his chest and mine. I almost couldn't believe someone could love me that much. I was in my late teens and he picked me up off the ground like I was a little baby. As we spent more time together I saw myself in him. Not only did we look so much alike. But even his yawn looked like mine. Simple gestures and body movements were nearly identical. As I've grown older the similarities have become more noticeable. And I've become more appreciative and thankful to know where and who I've come from. I hope every father and child recognise the significance they have to each other, that every parent and guardian realises this treasure. I certainly have and will forever cherish what I'd lost for a time in my life.

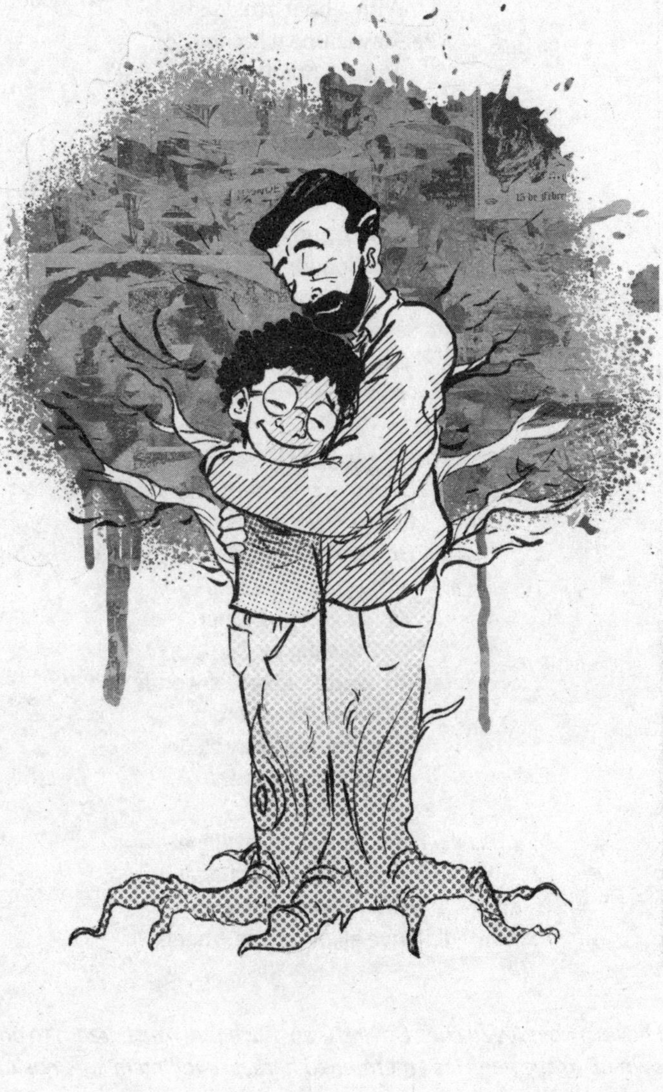

BIG WHEELS

Ferrari Testarossa I could toast to that
Range Rover on the coast
With a boat attached
Bentley coupe with no roof
With no holding back
If I could own my favourite cars
I'd roll over the whole map
I could do with an Aston Martin
Push a Porsche past the margins
Charge up my Tesla
Set my destination and my targets
Fill all their tanks
And see which goes the farthest
Captain my own fleet
A garage full of starships

I would get gone like a Giannini
Driving my Lamborgini
Range Rover Defender
A Hummer in the summer
Sitting by the sea
Shining as a stunner
Traveling by car
Seeing the world's greatest wonders
Camera on board
For pictures, videos
and album covers

I love cars and travelling
To me they're a big deal
With my poetic licence
I'd drive all of my big wheels

I have always loved cars. Driving is so much fun. And I dream to one day own all of the vehicles I mentioned here. Travelling in cars has always excited me because of the independence you have to go anywhere at any time. Seeing new places, meeting new people, and experiencing new cultures are extremely exciting parts of life. I can imagine waking up and driving to a new city everyday, writing, and performing poetry and music. It is said that travelling is one of the best ways to build intelligence. So this dream would benefit my brain as well. I've taken several big road trips in life. My family and I have driven from Los Angeles, California to Nevada, Las Vegas, from Kentucky to Florida, Kentucky to New Jersey, Kentucky to Oklahoma. Road trips are fun. To take them in these vehicles would be amazing.

Hue Man

Is that you man
Hue man
long legs and huge hands
wearing clothes
bright as peacocks and toucans

Is that you man
Hue man
cooking at food stands
with spice that smells nice
now I'm your food fan

Is that you man
in blue pants
doing that new dance
I've never seen before
got me moving to new jams

It is you
big and tall
short and round
thin and small
dancing to life's rhythms
How they move us all
I see joy on your face
I hear those laughs out loud
I don't understand your words
But I understand your smile
I feel what you feel
that connection in a crowd
connected as a vine
projecting out of the ground

I see you throwing shapes
yours square
mine round
They work well together
like base and treble sounds

So turn it up a little bit
I want to hear each part
every instrument's sounds
is a colour in art
I don't want to miss a beat
From California to Japan
I knew I recognised you
That's Hue Man

Variety is the spice of life. What makes our world amazing is its diversity. The distinguishing factor of our planet Earth to the others of our solar system is the wide range of life and environments we have. I think it is actually impossible to imagine Earth and life any other way. I was fortunate to grow up around many different cultures, Chinese, Italian, Jamaican, Puerto Rican, Polish, Jewish, African American, European, and Latino to name a few. This kept life very interesting. We were always learning new things. Today I experience that same newness and appreciation for culture as I now live in London.

THE MOORS

In the town of Gigglemoor
were homes with simple doors
padded walls, long halls
above slippery floors
there were no shoes allowed
only bright socks were worn
and the only way to travel
was in ice skaters form
The moors were explorers
natural born performers
who lived by the rule
you must laugh to escape boredom
So their door bell rings
were of lions grumpy and roaring
well partly that
with a mix of wordy snoring
Saying a true chuckle from the gut
causes bubbles to erupt
any troubles on the cusp
from sharp laughter
they would bust
and you weren't allowed to leave
until you laughed at least once
with big tears in your eyes
your stomach feeling the crunch
You silly billy soggy sausage
You must laugh until you've lost it
let it out fast
push past any caution
we want to see your dimples
you blushing until you're coughing
rushing through your words
fumbling while you're talking
loving the liberty of your laughing
is something that's really awesome
until you become addicted
and have to do it so often

So now how do you feel
light as feathers in the field
now you can float home
with the wind at your heels
If you didn't know it then
then I bet you know it now
laughter is the best medicine
In town
You're always welcome
To the Moors

This is my first fictitious silly story poem. I've been wanting to write one for a while. And am going to develop this writing style and content. It's good to try different approaches and humorous, funny ones as well. The Moors are a group of people who love to laugh and won't allow any around them not to. They know the power of laughter and have benefitted from it on all their travels around the world. So they've now set up a town with the laws of laughter. This story is to be continued.

PITCH PERFECT

They are world renowned
They resonate with any crowd
Conductors raising voices
From people so loud
From the fanciest footwork
And toes that twinkle
As keys to cities
Creating victory songs and jingles
Got em singing
Can you pass it like Pele
Or leave em messy like Messi
Give em the drama of Maradona
Or Ronaldinho is his hay day
Make balls take off
Like skyrockets toward the heavens
With either foot
Off the Portuguese CR7
Leave em seeing rainbows
Like the Neymar flick
Got em dancing to every move
Like Zidane's hips
If you wanna see a star

Well they are in their kit
Out of this world
When you see their kicks

The Maradona Cruyff turn
Slicing the air with the scissors
The Rabona, the Elastico,
Double step over to deliver,
A pass then pullback, and sea dribble like a fisher
Scorpion kick to sting opponents make em shiver
That's the definition of a baller

Dribbling, passing, trapping, with body control,
shooting with great precision
That's the mind of the pros
When you see it live
It inspires your soul
They make the pitch perfect
Got everyone singing out Goal….!!!

Living in London and my son now playing football has made me appreciate football more. All of my siblings played it. But I was the only one that didn't. At the time I thought it was too much running. But I've grown to appreciate all of the other wonderful aspects of it as sport regarding similar physical skills to the sports I love and have played. I love the abilities of all the players I've mentioned and many more. Being exposed to a variety of experiences makes life wonderful and interesting.

SHE RULES

I stood behind my words
They shielded me from fear
In time they grew sharper
They became a sword and a spear
Because she had shown me
How to use them
How to tune my ears
So my voice became a weapon
The more it became clear
She said the more you read
The more you'll see
What you couldn't unlock before
You'll soon set free
She taught us creative writing
She taught us history
She taught us science fiction
She taught us mystery
She taught us Frankenstein
She taught us Sherlock Holmes
She taught us English
She taught us poems
She taught me to express anger
She taught me there are songs
She taught me things I didn't know
I didn't learn on my own
She taught us to listen
She taught us to talk
She taught us the value
Of our own hearts

Teachers are very unique people. They devote the majority of their lives to caring for and empowering others, they have never known and may not ever personally benefit from, to fulfil their potential. It's hard to imagine giving so much of yourself away with no guarantee of a return. But teachers do and I suspect they do get a return when they see students learn what they teach. I could see this in my freshman year of high school with my English teacher Mrs. Polsgrove.

She was funny and easy to talk to. We the students wanted to be around her. I hadn't really worked on coming up with my own ideas until I started writing in her class. It was the reading that actually started it. It was the novel 'Frankenstein' that we were assigned to read. It was and is the story of a scientist that created a being that he couldn't control. We eventually discussed how this story could be a metaphor for how society impacts individuals by influencing them to think and behave in certain ways that over time become uncontrollable. I had never read anything in that way, metaphorically comparing life, novels or any creative writing. It forever changed how I read and write to this day. Teachers are some of the most significance contributors to our lives.